Torn

Back

Together

Areatae N. McGhee

I can be an open book or a closed door you make that happen with your actions.

~QUEEN~

Publication Page

Contact information:

Areatae McGhee
PO Box 1096
Mesa, AZ 85211

Torn Back Together
ISBN-10:0-9962813-2-0
ISBN-13: 978-0-9962813-2-4
www.inspire2byou.com
Twitter: @AuthorAreatae

Acknowledgement

To anyone who thought loving someone was easy, tough, exciting, hard work, emotional and butterflies.

You're right it's all of that.

Dedication

Momma Mary

Thank you for showing me how to love unconditionally.

Loving & missing you

Torn Back Together

You can't deny love when it's the reason

you got back together.

~QUEEN~

Strange Isn't It

Strange thing is

I had good intentions to be there

I had good intentions to support you

I made time in my schedule

I had a fight with my brain and heart

My mind wanted to compare

My heart skipped a beat when your name
came across my phone

I was afraid of what would become of it all

I stepped back

I had good intentions

When your name stopped coming across my
phone

Strange thing is

That's when I realized I had feelings for you

Strange isn't it?

Text Me

I had to give away your "Good Morning" text to someone else

Who replied back each time & if not before right after; told me to have a good morning too.

I had to give away your "Good Afternoon" text to someone else. Hope your day is going well text. The other person replied back that made me smile.

I have to give away your "Goodnight" text to someone else because each time I sent a text I got a reply back which reassured me they wanted to take this further.

Their intentions with me were very clear & put a smile on my face before bedtime.

Not only that, as soon as I would send the text saying goodnight. Ten minutes later a caller saying, I need to hear your voice.

Now when you text me here is my response:

"Someone got your Good Morning, Good Afternoon, and Goodnights, forever. I think you have the wrong number".

That Type

We caught eyes, and I'm feeling those
butterflies fly,

   type

One who calls my phone and tells me I'm in
his dreams, type

I place on hold, and he's still on the phone
when I come back 20 minutes later, type

Babe, Babe, call me back on my voicemail
like it's important,

   type

Wrap his arms around me on the steps of my
house when I'm going thru some family
issues,   type

Waiting in front of the house making sure I
got inside,

   type

Joke with you and laugh, type

Hold the door, type

Open up to vent to me about work and life,
type

Stay up all night and fall asleep on the phone,
type

Get a ride from your boy to my house and talk
to me thru the window,

type

Walks in the club with his boys and pulls me
to the side from my girls and whispers in my
ear, type

After the club tell my girls, I'm coming with
him, type

Make sure I eat, get my hair done and outfit,
type

I keep him fly, haircut, favorite cologne- fresh
kicks,

type

When I'm feeling down come over and hold me
in his arms,

type

Call to check on me when I'm going thru it,
type

I send him an encouraging text when we ain't
even talked,

        type

I know how he feels, I don't say a word just
hold him in my arms,

        type

Make sure he's encouraged and supported
when walks out our door and comes back
home, type

Hold my hands and pray we gone get thru it,
type

Talk about vacations and faraway places, but
know we paying off bills, type

Understands this is building a friendship, but
neither one of us are in the friendship box,

        type

When I fall asleep on the couch, he wakes me
up to get in the bed, type

In bed we cuddle and rub our feet together,
type

Run his hands thru my hair when kissing me,
type

Kissing me and kissing me,   type

Look me in my eyes and tell me I'm beautiful,
type

Upset and mad, but still come to get in the
bed, type

Never turn away, type

Understand we built this foundation, and it
can't be broke,

                    type

I have your heart, you have my heart, chapel,

doves,

      preacher,

                  vows and ring,

                              type

of love.

Be OVER it all

Or stay UNDER it forever

~QUEEN~

LOVE

I was told once I fall in love

I would drive hundreds of miles every chance I'd get to see him.

I'm driving

Lack Thereof

We both lack how to communicate on so many levels

There is no way I can understand what you're saying when I'm cutting you off and jumping in at the point you bring a subject up like I can't speak on it.

There is no way we can communicate when you don't listen. Yelling at me, talking over me when you asked me a question, and telling me to give you an explanation at the same time doesn't work.

There is no a way we are communicating on what matters to me through a text message. The emoji's & capital letter you use pisses me off. HOW DARE YOU YELL AT ME.? WHY DONT YOU ANSWER THE PHONE, but text me essays? It doesn't make sense.

There is no way we are communicating through a text message if I get a chance to respond to the last 3 text messages you send 5 more.

This can't be in real time

I just sent 4 text messages back and you're on another subject.

The only way we can communicate is by having conversations in person or picking up the phone so that we can listen each other.

I left for a reason. ~QUEEN~

The Gap

I didn't even know I was pulling away

> You too?

I see myself, but I tried to stay I did

The gap wasn't that big, so of course, we could have worked on it. Next, thing I know we're both thousands of miles away, and apart I felt the difference

It was just

d i s t a n c e

not a lost, so I am willing to travel to be back

talk back

come back to you

run back,

walk back

to get back to you

Next thing I know where thousands of miles away & we don't even speak.

Yes, the gap is that thick. Thick enough no one can cut through it. No fixing it for now because as long as time keeps going by and we don't speak the gap continues and just like me

I'm now out of reach.

Unapologetic

You told me everything about you, and I accepted you for who you are.

I enjoy your laughter; It always made me smile. I stop thinking about my status when you entered my heart.

I appreciated all your kind words when I lost my loved ones.

Very sweet, you stayed on my mind

You still do. You still are.

That smile, that laugh, gets me every time

I feel for you, just know your past didn't matter because each day is the present, and the present is all that means to me.

Conversations became more than the norm, and even though you say you don't want to be in a relationship,

                      you kiss me like you wanted to

held me like you wanted to

 listened to me as a relationship would do

We talked for hours about plans, family, life, weddings, etc. which you don't do if you're not interested in that,

type

And I still remember that night as if it was yesterday. I was open.

I got the best present months later. I am woman enough to accept my part in how things went down.

Like I said, the past is not here and now is the present. I've come this far

If this is another chance for us

To show we felt, Say what we should have said

Now is the time

I am all for speaking up for you. For us. I may communicate differently, but I still say the same thing.

I want you in my life, I support you, I love you, and we can build a beautiful life together.

You can only eat what your body craves.

LOYALTY

RESPECT

WORTH

LOVE

HONESTY

TRUST

APPREACTION

HEALTH

~QUEEN~

Thoughts of A Woman

Open the door and place my keys on the table.
I had a long day, and this eats me up more
and more. We need to have this talk......

I swear I'm not saying anything

No, No

I can't and I won't

The thing is .....Oh, never mind

You know what, I thought about it a million
times

Ok, today is the day

Damn, I'm over thinking this

Why is this so hard?

It's been 2 weeks, and I should have just told
him how I felt 2 weeks ago

I don't know why, but I'm afraid of the
response I would get back

Maybe, no response is needed at this time. It
might be a chance 4me to let it all out then it's
off my plate.

I would be free of all these butterflies, thoughts, and feelings I'm holding inside.

No, I didn't call or text

The more I wait, the more anxiety I get. How I feel right now, it doesn't matter the response. My need is to let it out.

My mind, body, and heart can't take it

It's now or never, and it has to be done. I'm going to call, no text, no email,

I will do it in person

Ok. Glad I thought that all the way through first.

Let's see what I can make for dinner.

I'm losing time trying to get to you, trying to close the gap, & the distance between us.
~QUEEN~

You're the only one I didn't choose, but my heart did.
~QUEEN~

Walk in your faith, not by sight. Wonder for a reason, and wave bye to those you have grown apart from.

Overcome the barriers and road block set in your path. Overlook the pettiness in others and work on the change in yourself.

Respect for your body, life, family, friends, associates. Be responsible for the people you let in your life and who you being into this world.

Time to learn who you are, visualize your plan and speak it into existence. Tailor your life & be Thankful in a positive way to stay ahead in whatever you do and not fall behind.

Humble yourself with life experiences. Honor thy mother, thy father & thy family. Help all three of your lifeline who stand by your side and give honest answers.

Alarm

It keeps going off, and you never hit the snooze button. I can never recall you turn it off because I always have to roll over you to do it.

Now I'm up before work. I always thought you did that to get breakfast

Wrinkled shirt

Smiles even when I'm half way sleep making breakfast. I'm thinking to myself; I could just run and grab something from the store and head to work. Who does this?

That's how much I was loved and cared

Tears

Ain't nothing like loving a man like you. Yes, you've had it rough, but so have I, but for some reason, you never acknowledge my struggle

Holding on

Making sure we are together in the eyes of God.

Prayer

And now that you're gone, I'm still waking up to the same alarm

Time

Rolling over on sheets that don't have you in them

Past tense

For some odd reason, I still butter toast and sit it in the same place

Non-sense

Because for once and forever, coming home to myself and learning to create beautiful world

My way

I got you, I just turned on the alarm

Set

The Porch

At the front of home doors

To be stood on, many sat on, on summer's days.

Naked on raining days, but in between changes of weather, the porch never moved.

Swept with a bristle stick broom many times the porch holds many conversations.

Thin lines and over the years or crisis times where we met.

 It catches the feelings as I wept day and night.

Footsteps walk by, and many conversations are held here. To sit here.

At the front of home doors.

In His Presence

In

    His

        Presence ....the world stops

Time doesn't change

The wind doesn't blow

And the birds outside stopping singing

The only thing moving is us

My arms around his body, his arms around mine as we greet

    At the door in an embrace

Feelings of warmth enter my body and the butterflies I had from his phone call

Began   to   f l y

Now in eternity I have all the time in the world for him

      To be mine

And for me

To be his

As we embrace .... we lay in bed

As he speaks, his first words are, hi.

My smile comes from

Down   within

As I reply back, Hi.

His hands, running through my hair now down to my arm and slowly caress my thigh.

I am open for the world has stopped.

We stare into each other's eyes as if we have known each other all our life.

Tiny kisses & pecks on the lips & face induces flames as I slide my legs in between his and he wraps his legs around mine

The world has stopped

Only he & I are here.

His fingers interlock with mine as we rub noses and giggle like little kids who have the last piece of candy & hide out to eat it together.

I take my hand & rub it thru his hair slow as I go in for a kiss....kiss...kiss, peck.....kiss kiss my body screams

Silently. As his body reacts, he grabs me tighter and kisses me back on

My neck....my neck...now down to my chest after while...............................

The world is no more

I heard melodies; the world no longer matters as millions of butterflies now turn into millions of flutters in my abdomen

The world isn't real I'm past cloud 9

When he is here in me, in his eyes clouds are all I can see.

The world can't compare to this

      We wake up   to move

Time for his presence to leave me and soon as I walk him to the door, I can hear the neighbors talking and traffic outside,

My last kiss & hug – words can't describe how I feel. Now, I hear everything as I release him from my arms to watch him leave. I hear everything; time is now back and has a priority,

The phone rings,

 I hear birds chirping.

The wind begins to blow

We let the world start moving again.

The door shuts.

Permission2

Love me without limits

    Yes, you have permission2

Give me a hug when you see me

    Yes, you have permission2

Show your feelings so I can reciprocate mine

    Yes, you have permission2

Be in my corner at all times

    Yes, you have permisson2

Be proud of who I am at all times

    Yes, you have permisson2

Take care of me

    Yes, you have permisson2

Find out what I like and use that to make me happy

I was afraid to tell you how I felt

I decided to tell you anyway

No matter, no matter

I could have held it in for another week,
month or year

Something in me

>   Just wanted to

>   Just needed to

>   Just had to

Let you know

Yes, you have permission to

be in my life forever.

Tear Drop

U

Need

To hold me

Hold me physically

And then keep me spiritually.

Then I know you can take me on.

I'm hard to deal with, loved by many,

Driven and can break at times, so I need

You to reassure me, yes me. You're the only

Thing I didn't choose but my heart,

In time my heart

Did.

Maybe

It was

The times you called when I was on my way to work

A good morning text

Your kiss

The way you would make me laugh

When you first told me you cared about me

Just maybe it was all of that

The calls to make sure I made it to work and home

The assignments you would help me with

Nights of talking about life and the future

Why would I let all of that go?

What My Heart Still Holds

I can't walk away

I'm thinking of no other

nobody can love me like you

I can't explain it

It's a feeling I can't touch.

I've tried others, and I've waited, but no other
has matched the way you make me feel.

"You still don't get it. Your fear of loving a
woman who knows her worth terrifies you."
~QUEEN~

If you're not ready to hang with people who make you accountable for your actions, you will never reach your destiny and you're not ready to live to be the true you. ~QUEEN~

Complete

Is it with you? Or the idea of you?

In my mind it makes sense, but to others, it's a complicated situation. Just as my heart beats you complete me.

I'm better with you than without you.

Doctors say, my health is better because your love makes me happy. And just like that, our time is embedded in my heart and mind.

Those who look in can't understand. Those who look out are the only one with a solution.

Like a whirlwind in the process of completion, you're a part of that cycle, that cycles through the land. Along the path, I'm picking up behaviors, thoughts, feelings for you and don't want to stop.

I'm complete with you.

  If I could

      Rewrite the past I would.

If I could

Rewrite the past I would.

If I could change everything, I wouldn't.

Maybe we would have never met.

I can apologize for my actions, we would be back together, or I can force the issue, but all I can do is try.

Love isn't enough; some people stop trying this and trying that

Complete

Is it with you?

Or the idea of you?

In my mind it makes sense, but to others it's a complicated situation.

www.ingramcontent.com/pod-product-compliance
Lightning Source LLC
Chambersburg PA
CBHW060628030426
42337CB00018B/3260